ISAAC ASIMOV'S NEW LIBRARY OF THE UNIVERSE

DEATH FROM SPACE: WHAT KILLED THE DINOSAURS?

BY ISAAC ASIMOV
WITH REVISIONS AND UPDATING BY GREG WALZ-CHOJNACKI

Gareth Stevens Publishing
MILWAUKEE

For a free color catalog describing Gareth Stevens' list of high-quality books, call 1-800-542-2595 (USA) or 1-800-461-9120 (Canada). Gareth Stevens' Fax: (414) 225-0377.

The publisher would like to thank Professor Martin Greenberg for his abundant energy, technical skill, and personal commitment to this project. Mr. Walz-Chojnacki would like to thank Drs. Ed Tagliaferri, David Tholen, and Paul Weissman for helpful discussion during the preparation of this edition.

Library of Congress Cataloging-in-Publication Data

Asimov, Isaac.
  Death from space: what killed the dinosaurs? / by Isaac Asimov and Greg Walz-Chojnacki.
    p. cm. — (Isaac Asimov's New library of the universe)
  Rev. ed. of: Did comets kill the dinosaurs? 1988.
  Includes index.
  ISBN 0-8368-1129-1
  1. Dinosaurs—Juvenile literature. [1. Dinosaurs. 2. Extinction (Biology)] I. Walz-Chojnacki, Greg, 1954-. II. Asimov, Isaac. Did comets kill the dinosaurs? III. Title. IV. Series: Asimov, Isaac. New library of the universe.
  QE862.D5A76 1994
  567.9'1—dc20   94-15432

This edition first published in 1994 by
Gareth Stevens Publishing
1555 North RiverCenter Drive, Suite 201
Milwaukee, Wisconsin 53212, USA

Project editor: Barbara J. Behm
Design adaptation: Helene Feider
Editorial assistant: Diane Laska
Production director: Susan Ashley
Picture research: Kathy Keller
Artwork commissioning: Kathy Keller and Laurie Shock

Printed in the United States of America

1 2 3 4 5 6 7 8 9 99 98 97 96 95 94

To bring this classic of young people's information up to date, the editors at Gareth Stevens Publishing have selected two noted science authors, Greg Walz-Chojnacki and Francis Reddy. Walz-Chojnacki and Reddy coauthored the recent book *Celestial Delights: The Best Astronomical Events Through 2001.*

Walz-Chojnacki is also the author of the book *Comet: The Story Behind Halley's Comet* and various articles about the space program. He was an editor of *Odyssey*, an astronomy and space technology magazine for young people, for eleven years.

Reddy is the author of nine books, including *Halley's Comet, Children's Atlas of the Universe, Children's Atlas of Earth Through Time*, and *Children's Atlas of Native Americans*, plus numerous articles. He was an editor of *Astronomy* magazine for several years.

CONTENTS

We live in an enormously large place – the Universe. It's just in the last fifty-five years or so that we've found out how large it probably is. It's only natural that we would want to understand the place in which we live, so scientists have developed instruments – such as radio telescopes, satellites, probes, and many more – that have told us far more about the Universe than could possibly be imagined.

We have seen planets up close. We have learned about quasars and pulsars, black holes, and supernovas. We have gathered amazing data about how the Universe may have come into being and how it may end. Nothing could be more astonishing.

Facts about the Universe aren't always about the faraway. Right here on Earth, there were once giant animals called dinosaurs. About 65 million years ago, they disappeared. The reason why they vanished might be found in outer space. Out there we may discover not only the secret of the dinosaurs' end, but also learn about dangers that could threaten our Earth in the future. By learning more about space, we will hopefully be able to escape those dangers.

Isaac Asimov

Days of the Dinosaurs

Once, millions of years ago, large animals called dinosaurs walked on Earth. Some of them were up to 90 feet (27.4 meters) long. Some may have weighed as much as 100 tons or more – equal to about twelve elephants. The largest dinosaurs were plant-eaters, but the dinosaur pictured here is a meat-eater, the most terrifying dinosaur that ever lived. It is a *Tyrannosaurus*. It was nearly 50 feet (15.2 m) long and was heavier than most elephants. Its head was up to 5 feet (1.5 m) long, and each of its teeth could be over 7 inches (17.8 centimeters) long.

? *Were some dinosaurs warm blooded?*

Some scientists believe the dinosaurs were reptiles. They can tell that from the structure of dinosaur bones. All the reptiles that are alive now – turtles, lizards, snakes, alligators – are cold blooded. This means that when the weather is cold, they are cold, too, and become very sluggish and slow in their movements.

But other scientists are sure that certain dinosaurs were quite active in the cold. These scientists believe some of the dinosaurs were warm blooded. After all, birds and mammals are descended from reptiles, and they are warm blooded. So far, there is no way to tell for certain if some of the dinosaurs were warm blooded.

Left: If people had lived in the state of Montana when *Tyrannosaurus* did, this dinosaur could have swallowed them whole.

Mighty Rulers of Earth

The dinosaurs first evolved about 225 million years ago. For 140 million years, they ruled Earth. Some kinds died out, and others came into being. Then, around 65 million years ago, they all died out. All we have left as evidence of these prehistoric beings are bones, teeth, footprints, and fossils.

Why did the dinosaurs die? Scientists have wondered if the climate changed, if small animals began eating dinosaur eggs, or if a nearby exploding star showered Earth with deadly X rays.

! *Ultraheavy . . . ultralong . . . ultratall: it's* **Ultrasaurus!**

The largest known land animal of all time was a dinosaur called Ultrasaurus. *The few bones discovered so far tell scientists that the animal must have weighed 100-140 tons and measured 100-115 feet (30-35 m) long and about 56 feet (17 m) tall — about three times as tall as a giraffe. This means it would have been as tall as a five-story house.*

Right: The size and depth of a footprint can reveal how much a dinosaur weighed.

Far right: These dinosaur fossils are in a quarry wall that was once under the ground.

6

Mysterious Encounter

In 1978, scientists found a layer of rare material called iridium in rocks that were about 65 million years old. There was more iridium in rocks this age than in others. Iridium is not usually found in rocks on Earth. It is more common in materials from outer space. Where did the iridium come from? Possibly it came from meteoroids, which are rocks that move through space and sometimes collide with Earth as meteorites. Before they hit Earth, they enter the atmosphere as fiery meteors. The large ones leave a crater, or hole, where they land. Some craters are so old they have worn away, but scientists can detect signs of these craters when doing research from the air.

Top photos: One of the world's most beautiful craters is in western Australia. It is called the Wolf Creek Crater.

Bottom: The Barringer Meteor Crater in Arizona is about 3/4 mile (1.2 kilometers) across. Scientists think it was created by a meteorite impact fifty thousand years ago.

With dust blocking the Sun's heat and light, Earth would have become cold and dark. These kinds of conditions would have killed off most plants and animals.

A World Gone Cold and Dark

Could something that struck Earth 65 million years ago have killed the dinosaurs? It could have. One possibility is that if the object was big enough, it could have gouged out a huge quantity of rock and soil, ground it into dust, and flung that dust high in the air for miles and miles. The dust would have spread throughout Earth. It would have blocked the sunlight. Little light or heat would have reached Earth for months, or even years. The plants would have died, and then large animals, such as dinosaurs that ate plants or other animals, would have died. Smaller animals might have nibbled at bark or seeds, or eaten the frozen bodies of larger animals. Some of the smaller animals would have survived. But the dinosaurs would have all died out.

On a Collision Course?

Are there large objects in space that could possibly hit Earth? Yes. So far, scientists have detected a couple of dozen objects with a diameter of 1 mile (1.6 km) or more that currently come within a few million miles of Earth. There may be more than a thousand of these in all. Although, at present, they are a safe distance away from Earth, the gravitational pull of planets can change the paths of these objects.

There is a possibility that one of these objects, on a changed path, might crash into us one day —just as an object from space may have crashed into Earth 65 million years ago!

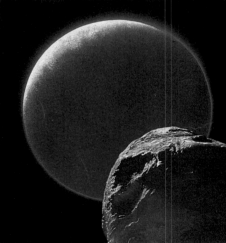

Top: Some comets and asteroids travel dangerously close to Earth. In this picture, the paths of these comets are in yellow, and the paths of these asteroids are in red. Earth is indicated with an arrow.

Bottom collage: Lured by Earth's gravitational pull, a meteoroid approaches our prehistoric Earth *(upper left)* and enters the atmosphere as a fiery meteor *(lower left)*. Now a meteorite, it collides with Earth *(middle)* as a dinosaur watches *(right)*. Will this mean the end of the dinosaur's food supply?

Damage from High in the Sky

An object doesn't have to actually strike Earth's surface to do a lot of damage. If a comet or asteroid were to collide with Earth, it would probably hit at enormously high speeds. The pressure of speeding through the air could actually tear the object apart with an enormous explosion.

In 1908, an object from space supposedly struck the middle of Siberia. It knocked down every tree in an area more than 15 miles (25 km) across. But it didn't kill any people because people were not living there. The fallen trees can still be seen, but there is no crater. Scientists now realize that the damage was the result of the explosion of a small comet or asteroid high in the atmosphere.

Opposite: An icy comet vaporizes as it speeds toward Earth. Its destination – Siberia.

Inset: Siberia, the site of a possible comet strike in 1908 near the Tunguska River.

ГОРА „ОБЕДЕННАЯ" ВИД НА СЕВ

СПЛОШНОЙ ОРИЕНТИРОВАННЫЙ БУРЕЛОМ ПЛОЩАДИ

! Comets – a sign of doom?

In older times, people did not really know what comets were. They thought they were warnings from the heavens of upcoming disaster. After seeing a comet, they thought a war would come, a plague would rage, or a king would die. Of course, even when a comet didn't appear, terrible events like that happened. Somehow, people never seemed to consider that.

осток.

With the compliments of
The author
19 ⁷/₅ 29.
Z.Kulik

0-15 км от центральной

The View from Space – It's a Blast!

Between 1975 and 1992, spy satellites launched by the United States government observed 136 explosions (about 8 each year) high in the atmosphere throughout the world. The explosions were the size of small nuclear bombs, and they were created by small asteroids. Scientists think more of these explosions have occurred – perhaps as many as 80 a year.

The explosions were probably only about 50 feet (15 m) across. Most of them were much smaller than the Tunguska explosion and weren't even noticed from the ground. But one that occurred over the Pacific Ocean may have flashed as bright as the Sun.

Left: One recent explosion caused by an asteroid occurred above the Great Lakes area of the United States and is shown reflected in Lake Michigan. The lights of Chicago, Illinois, can be seen *on the left.*

Below: This map shows the locations of 136 explosions caused by small asteroids high in the atmosphere between 1975 and 1992. Maybe one occurred above your hometown!

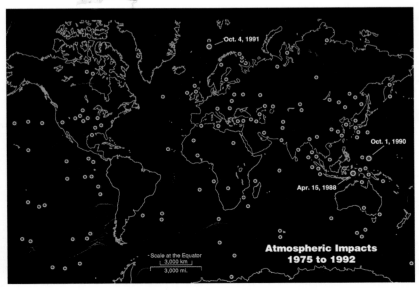

Oct. 4, 1991

Oct. 1, 1990

Apr. 15, 1988

Scale at the Equator
3,000 km
3,000 mi.

**Atmospheric Impacts
1975 to 1992**

The Cosmic Shooting Gallery

We know comets can hit planets because we saw it happen in 1994. In July of that year, a comet named Shoemaker-Levy collided with Jupiter. The comet hit the far side of the planet. As the planet turned, astronomers could see the spots where the comet hit just a few hours before!

Opposite: Shoemaker-Levy striking Jupiter.

Below, top: This picture of Shoemaker-Levy shows that it is actually in several different pieces, pulled apart by Jupiter's strong gravity.

Below, bottom: Jupiter's moons often get in the way of comet bombardment. The craters on Jupiter's moon Callisto were probably created by a string of comets like Shoemaker-Levy.

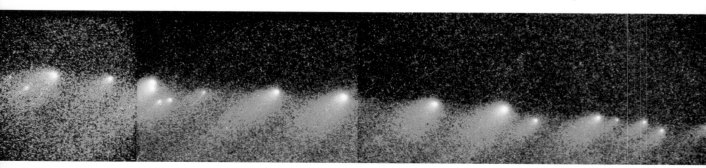

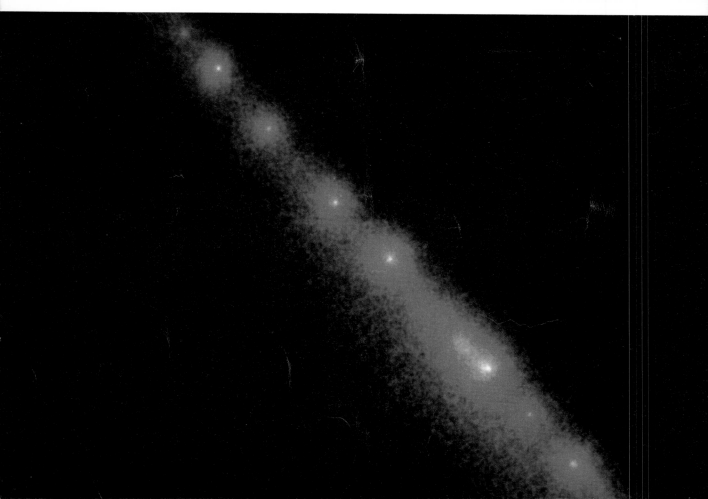

Ground Zero – Found!

Could scientists find the crater of an object that hit Earth 65 million years ago? The surface of the planet can change a great deal in all that time, and many old craters have disappeared as mountains have grown and the oceans have changed the craters' shapes.

But geophysicists, scientists who study Earth's features, have found signs of an enormous crater in the Yucatan Peninsula of Mexico. The crater is invisible to the eye, but using special instruments, scientists have detected a crater that is just the right size and age to be the one created when the dinosaurs disappeared.

After years of searching, scientists now believe they know exactly where a comet or asteroid struck Earth, setting off the chain of events that probably wiped out the dinosaurs.

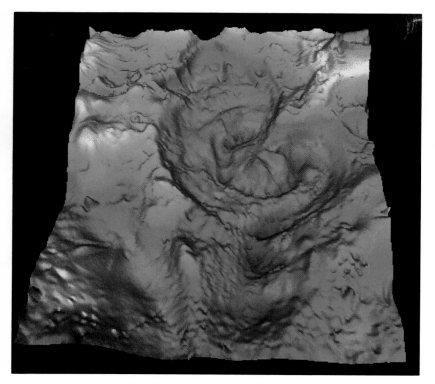

Opposite, top: The crater in the Yucatan Peninsula in Mexico, whose impact probably led to the demise of the dinosaurs, is half on land and half in the water. Besides blocking out the Sun, the impact caused a colossal wave that reached several hundred miles (km) away.

Opposite, bottom: This illustration shows the location of a buried crater that was caused by a comet or asteroid strike on Earth 65 million years ago. This probably led to the extinction of the dinosaurs. The circular feature, called the Cenote Ring, provides surface evidence of the buried crater's exact location and size.

Left: The various colors in this picture show tiny differences in gravity in the Yucatan Peninsula. These differences are arranged in a circular pattern, forming a ring 110 miles (180 km) across. This "gravity ring" is caused by material piled up by a huge impact at the site 65 million years ago.

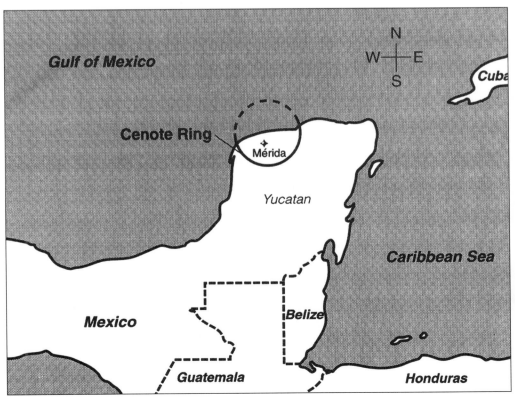

The Oort Cloud – the Beginning

Although comets do not get as large as asteroids, they often travel much faster. If a comet were large enough, it would punch right through the atmosphere and gouge out a crater like the one found in Mexico. Some scientists think it definitely was a comet, not an asteroid, that led to the death of the dinosaurs. A Dutch astronomer, Jan Oort, believed there are many billions of comets slowly orbiting the Sun many times farther away than the planets. This "Oort cloud" might be where Earth-colliders start their journey.

Left: Comets in the Oort cloud. The gravity of passing stars may pull some of these comets out of the Oort cloud and into Earth's orbit.

? *Comets – a look back in time?*

The Sun and the planets formed out of a cloud of dust and gas. We cannot be sure what the cloud was made of. In the billions of years in which the Solar System has existed, the Sun and the planets have changed a great deal. On Earth, for instance, some of the original matter has been lost to space, and some has sunk to the center of Earth. Scientists think comets are samples of the original cloud that have not changed with the years. That is one reason researchers were so excited when spacecraft passed near Halley's Comet in 1986. It was the first time a comet was studied up close. Further studies on comets may tell us more about the beginnings of our own Earth.

Clockwork Disasters?

Some scientists think that every 26 million years, like clockwork, comets from the Oort cloud hit Earth and cause different kinds of life-forms to die out. It isn't hard to imagine a large comet striking Earth. But what could cause collisions to occur, like clockwork, every 26 million years? Certain scientists have developed three theories, but many other scientists doubt that any of the theories are correct. In fact, most scientists do not believe that comets strike Earth in regular showers at all.

Below: One theory – perhaps the Sun has a small companion star. Such a star could pass through the Oort cloud, sending comets toward Earth.

Opposite, top: A second theory – as it orbits the Galaxy, the Sun follows a slightly wavy path, first above the midline of the Galaxy, then below it. Every time the Sun passes through the midline, a stronger gravitational pull could send comets toward Earth.

Opposite, bottom: A third theory – there may be a distant, unknown planet with a wobbly orbit that travels through the Oort cloud every 26 million years. This might knock comets toward Earth.

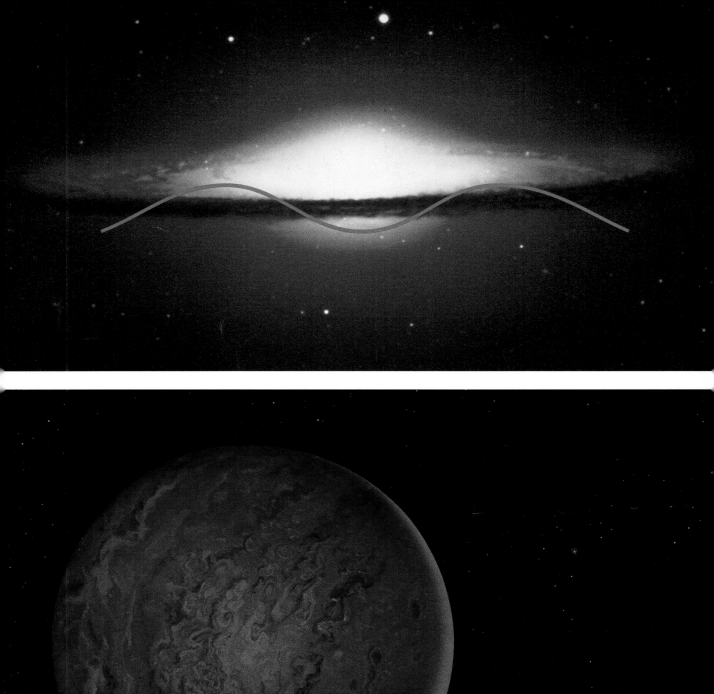
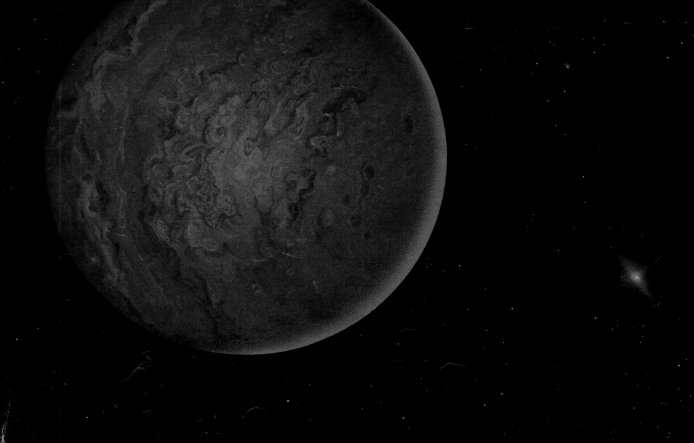

Diverting Disaster

If the theory of collisions every 26 million years turns out to be correct, Earth is about halfway in time between major comet strikes. Earth might be hit by a body from space at any time, of course. But the real danger may not come for another 13 million years.

Will that be the end of human beings? Maybe not. By that time, we should have colonies on various bodies in the Solar System, and we should have cities built in space.

Wherever we are, we could be watching for the approach of any dangerous body. We could push it aside, or even destroy it with advanced technology. Then we'd be sure that no collision from outer space could kill *us* the way it killed the dinosaurs.

Top: If comets are going to hit Earth in just 13 million years, maybe we should plan to be in space when they arrive! NASA scientists and engineers have designed permanent colonies for use in space. These colonies could be on other planets, such as Mars, or in outer space itself. This colony looks like a giant wheel *(left)*. A large mirror *(right)* directs sunlight into the colony.

Right: This space colony would be home to ten thousand people 250,000 miles (402,000 km) from Earth. It would be constructed out of ore mined from the Moon.

Far right: If you look carefully, you will see that this proposed space colony has a bridge like the Golden Gate Bridge in San Francisco, California. In this picture, city lights are reflected in the large, mirrored panels that direct sunlight into the colony.

Fact File: What Killed the Dinosaurs?
Why Did the Dinosaurs and Other Prehistoric Reptiles Die Out?

Possible Causes	Possible Effects
Changes in climate	Some types of plants disappeared, leaving some dinosaurs without food
Small animals eating dinosaur eggs	Fewer dinosaurs reaching adulthood and reproducing
Major catastrophes or natural disruptions on Earth, such as the rise of mountain chains, huge floods, or volcanic eruptions	Sudden death of plant and animal life
An asteroid or a very large meteorite striking Earth	Dust thrown out from the impact – blocking out light and heat from the Sun for months or years, killing plants and causing large animals that ate plants or other animals to die, too
Comet strike (Scientists now believe that this actually may have happened.)	Life-forms die out – the kinds and numbers would depend on how much damage done by comet
A nearby star exploding	Earth showered with deadly X rays

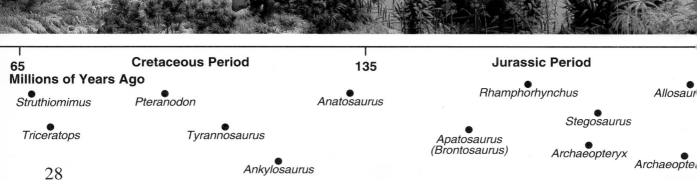

65   **Cretaceous Period**   135   **Jurassic Period**
Millions of Years Ago

Struthiomimus   Pteranodon   Anatosaurus   Rhamphorhynchus   Allosaur

Stegosaurus

Triceratops   Tyrannosaurus   Apatosaurus (Brontosaurus)   Archaeopteryx   Archaeopte

Ankylosaurus

A Pictorial Walk through Prehistory

Take a pictorial walk through prehistory. Our walk begins at the left, 65 million years ago. This is when dinosaurs disappeared from the face of Earth. Our walk ends at the far right, some 400 million years ago, before the Age of Reptiles began.

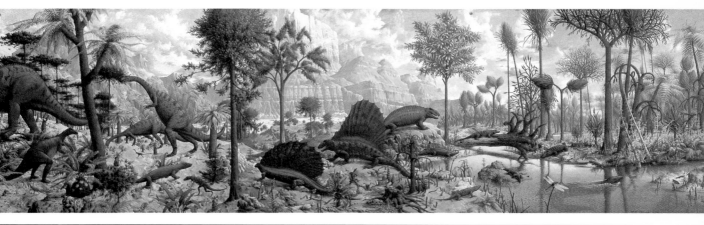

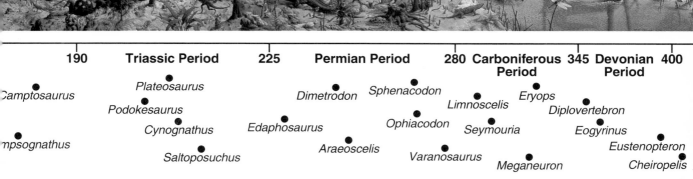

190 **Triassic Period** 225 **Permian Period** 280 **Carboniferous** 345 **Devonian** 400
Period **Period**

Camptosaurus

Plateosaurus

Podokesaurus

Dimetrodon Sphenacodon

Eryops

Limnoscelis

Diplovertebron

Edaphosaurus

Ophiacodon Seymouria

Eogyrinus

Cynognathus

Araeoscelis

mpsognathus

Varanosaurus

Eustenopteron

Saltoposuchus

Meganeuron

Cheiropelis

More Books about Comets and Dinosaurs

Comets and Meteors. Fichter (Franklin Watts)
How Did We Find Out about Comets? Asimov (Avon)
How Did We Find Out about Dinosaurs? Asimov (Avon)
The Last Days of the Dinosaurs. Gabriele (Penny Lane)
Last of the Dinosaurs, the End of an Age. Eldridge (Troll)
The New *Dinosaur Collection.*   (Gareth Stevens)

Video

Comets and Meteors. (Gareth Stevens)

Places to Visit

You can explore the comets and other fascinating parts of the Universe without leaving Earth. Here are some museums and centers where you can find a variety of space exhibits.

NASA Lewis Research Center
Educational Services Office
21000 Brookpark Road
Cleveland, OH 44135

Field Museum of Natural History (dinosaurs)
Roosevelt Road at Lake Shore Drive
Chicago, IL 60605

Astrocentre
Royal Ontario Museum
100 Queen's Park
Toronto, Ontario M5S 2C6

Hayden Planetarium
Museum of Science
Science Park
Boston, MA 02114-1099

Edmonton Space and Science Centre
11211 - 142nd Street
Edmonton, Alberta K5M 4A1

Perth Observatory
Walnut Road
Bickley, W.A. 6076 Australia

Places to Write

Here are some places you can write for more information about comets. Be sure to state what kind of information you would like. Include your full name and address so they can write back to you.

National Space Society
922 Pennsylvania Avenue SE
Washington, D.C. 20003

NASA Kennedy Space Center
PA-ESB
Kennedy Space Center, FL 32899

Sydney Observatory
P. O. Box K346
Haymarket 2000 Australia

Department of Industry
235 Queen Street
Ottawa, Ontario K1A 0H5

Glossary

asteroid: a small, rocky body in orbit around the Sun. Most asteroids lie between Mars and Jupiter, but there are thousands that travel near Earth.

billion: the number represented by 1 followed by nine zeroes – 1,000,000,000. In some countries, this number is called "a thousand million." In these countries, one billion would then be represented by 1 followed by twelve zeroes – 1,000,000,000,000: a million million.

cold blooded: having blood that changes temperature according to the temperature of the surroundings.

colony: a group of people settled in a place away from their original home.

comet: an object made of ice, rock, and gas; a comet has a vapor tail that may be seen when the comet's orbit is close to the Sun.

crater: a hole in the ground caused by the impact of an object from space striking Earth.

evolve: to develop or change over a long period of time.

galaxy: a huge group of stars and their satellites, as well as gas and dust. A galaxy might have tens of billions of stars. The Milky Way is our Galaxy.

geophysicist: a scientist who studies the features of Earth.

gravity: the force that causes objects like Earth and our Moon to be attracted to one another.

iridium: a rare element that occurs more in extra-terrestrial objects than in Earth's crust.

meteor: a meteoroid that has entered Earth's atmosphere.

meteorite: what is left of a meteoroid once it hits Earth.

meteoroid: a tiny piece of rock or dust in orbit around the Sun. When one of these objects strikes Earth's atmosphere, it streaks through the sky as a meteor.

NASA: the space agency of the United States – the National Aeronautics and Space Administration.

Solar System: our Planetary System – the Sun with the planets and all other bodies that orbit the Sun.

Tyrannosaurus: a terrifying, meat-eating dinosaur.

Ultrasaurus: the largest known land animal of all time.

vaporize: to turn something that is liquid or solid into a gas.

warm blooded: having blood that stays about the same temperature regardless of the changing temperature of the surroundings.

Index

Born in 1920, Isaac Asimov came to the United States as a young boy from his native Russia. As a young man, he was a student of biochemistry. In time, he became one of the most productive writers the world has ever known. His books cover a spectrum of topics, including science, history, language theory, fantasy, and science fiction. His brilliant imagination gained him the respect and admiration of adults and children alike. Sadly, Isaac Asimov died shortly after the publication of the first edition of *Isaac Asimov's Library of the Universe*.

The publishers wish to thank the following for permission to reproduce copyright material: front cover, © Julian Baum; 4-5, Rudolf Zallinger, Peabody Museum of Natural History; 6-7, Terry Huseby, © *Discover* Magazine (March 1986); 8, 8-9 (upper), Georg Gerster, Science Source; 8-9 (lower), © Allan E. Morton; 10-11, 12 (both), © Julian Baum; 12-13, © Mark Paternostro; 13 (both), © Julian Baum; 14-15, Leonid Kulik, courtesy of Smithsonian Institution; 15, © Mark Paternostro; 16-17, © Michael Carroll 1994; 17, José R. Díaz, *Sky & Telescope* Magazine, © 1993 Sky Publishing Corp.; 18 (upper), NASA/JPL; 18 (lower), Dr. H. A. Weaver and Mr. T. E. Smith, STScI/NASA; 19, NASA/JPL; 20, © V. L. Sharpton/Lunar and Planetary Institute; 21 (upper), © Ron Miller; 21 (lower), NASA; 22-23, 24, © Mark Paternostro; 25 (upper), Courtesy of European Southern Observatory; 25 (lower), © Michael Carroll; 26-27 (all), NASA; 28-29, Rudolf Zallinger, Peabody Museum of Natural History.